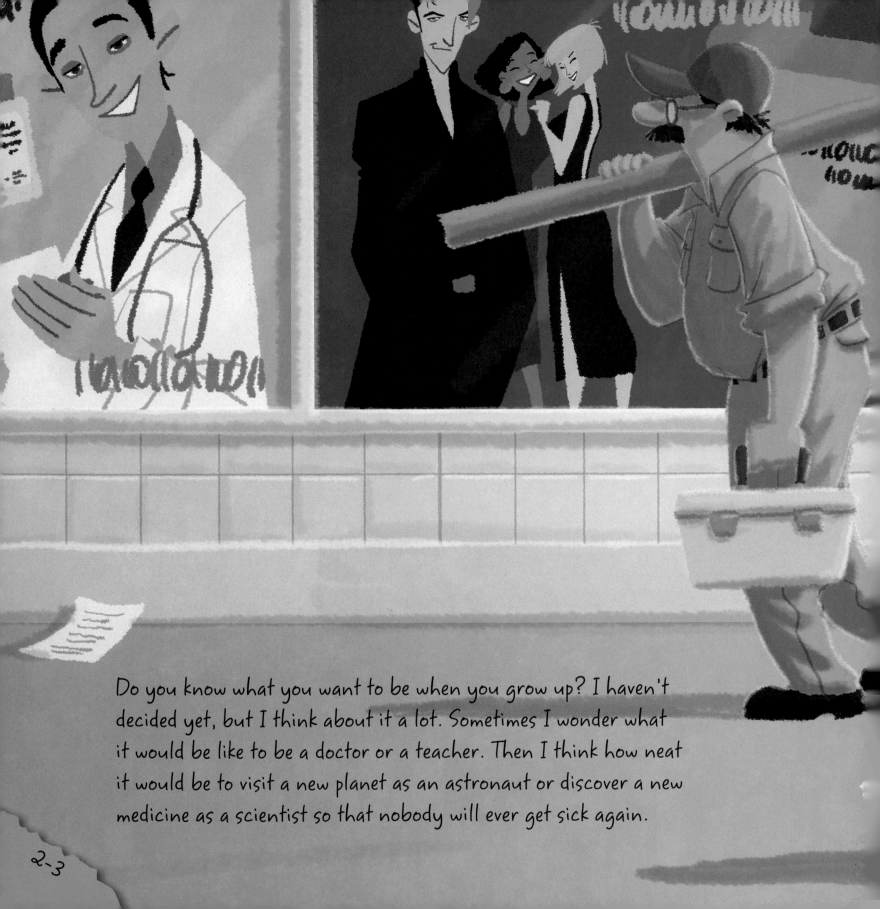

Do you know what you want to be when you grow up? I haven't decided yet, but I think about it a lot. Sometimes I wonder what it would be like to be a doctor or a teacher. Then I think how neat it would be to visit a new planet as an astronaut or discover a new medicine as a scientist so that nobody will ever get sick again.

Mom and Dad keep telling me that I can be anything I want to be as long as I work hard and do well at school. Mom said that part of my job as a kid is to go to school, study hard, and do the best I can. Then, when I get older, I can be anything I want, even an animal doctor.

6-7

I know that doing well at school is a good idea, but sometimes learning and studying aren't any fun at all! Sometimes they're boring and other times they're just way too hard!!!

8-9

Did you know that studying is a full-time job? There are projects to do, homework to finish, books to read, spelling tests, and math tests. And just when you think you've finished, there's always more. Another book report, another test to study for — it's endless!

So what does this mean? It means that there is less time to do fun things, like hanging out with friends or watching TV. Then, when there is time to have fun, everybody else is busy studying. Sometimes, don't you just want to quit studying so hard and just have fun? I know I do!

But then I think of all those times when I really studied hard for a test and I got an A. It's the best feeling in the world when that happens, and that's when missing my favorite TV show because I had to study doesn't seem so terrible anymore. Getting an A is worth it.

What do you like best about school besides recess and lunch? The part I like best about school is when we learn about something really cool like volcanoes or dinosaurs or when we learn how to play different kinds of instruments like the flute or the trumpet. That's when school and learning are fun!

But have you ever tried really hard to learn something new, but no matter how hard you tried, you just couldn't get it? I think this happens to everybody at least once in awhile. Whenever this happens to me, I get frustrated, and I just want to stop trying.

Last week, my teacher was showing the class a new way to do multiplication, but I just couldn't figure it out, no matter how hard I tried. After awhile, I got frustrated, and I wanted to give up, but my teacher wouldn't let me.

Instead, my teacher stayed after school and helped
me with my multiplication. I knew a test was coming up,
and it was important for me to learn the math. Although
I didn't want to miss walking home with my friends,
I did! While my friends left to go home, I was stuck
with my teacher in the classroom! Ugh!

20-21

The surprising part about staying after school with my teacher was that I had fun. My teacher showed me some different ways to learn and some fun ways to study. By the time I left, not only was I laughing and joking around with my teacher, but I had also finally figured out multiplication. I got it!

A few days later, when it was time for me to take the multiplication test, I was scared. I didn't want to let down my teacher, my parents, or myself. I wanted to prove to everybody that I could do it. When the teacher handed out the test and the class was told to begin, my head went blank and I couldn't remember anything. I started to get scared!

For a few minutes, I sat and watched the kids around me working on their tests. Then, out of the corner of my eye, I saw my teacher looking at me. When I looked over at her and she smiled and gave me a thumbs up, that's when I remembered all the things I had studied. I picked up my pencil and started the test.

And guess what? I did it! I got a B+ on that test. All my studying and hard work was worth it because not only did it feel great to get a good grade, but I also learned that studying doesn't have to be so hard. There's more than one way to study, and when you make studying fun, learning is easy!

Parents Guide

Here are a few suggestions to help make studying a little bit more enjoyable:

Design Your Own Thinking Hat

All you need are a few sheets of newspaper and some tape. However, for those of you who like a little color, don't forget the marker pens, glitter glue, stickers, and even some artificial flowers.

Place 2–3 sheets of newspaper on your head and mold the paper around the top of your head in order to shape the top of the hat. Ask an adult to place tape all around the newspaper just above your eyebrows in order to keep the shape of your hat. Then crumple the edge of the paper all around to form the rim. For those of you who like flowers, glue a few flowers on the rim of your hat. Now it's time to get thinking!

Flash Cards

They are perfect for practicing math and spelling and for helping you to learn some quick facts. All you need is a pile of index cards and some markers. On each index card, write down what you need to learn. And there you have it! And guess what? Not only will this make learning easy, but also, while taking the time to make your flash cards, you are actually studying!

What better way to make studying time fun?

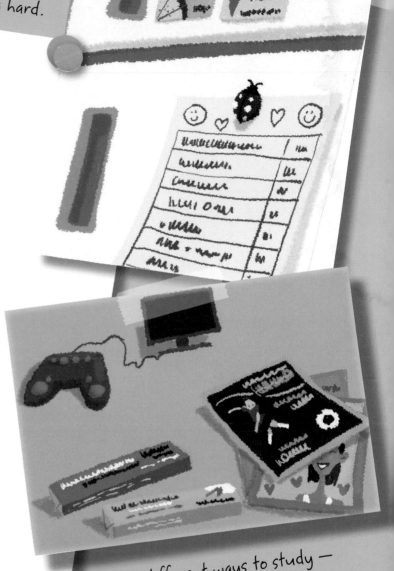

Penny For Your Thoughts!
Yes, getting good grades should be enough of a reward; however, sometimes a little extra motivation doesn't hurt — in fact, it might be needed.

The first step is to decide with your child what he or she needs to do in order to earn a reward. Then write down what you have decided on a piece of construction paper and post it in an area that is visible to everybody. That way, everybody is on the same page.

For example, staying at the table until all homework is completed earns a certain reward. Getting a good grade on a test earns a better reward. If your child is really struggling with completing his or her homework or preparing for his or her test, you may want to reward the effort in trying to do the homework or study for the test.

A reward could be stickers, extra television time, a popsicle, a pack of gum, or the like.

Try different ways to study — mix things up!

Remember, reward the behavior you want to see more of.

Studying is hard

First edition for the United States, its territories and dependencies, and Canada published in 2013 by Barron's Educational Series, Inc.

© Copyright 2012 by Gemser Publications, S.L.
El Castell, 38, 08329 Teià, Barcelona, Spain

Text: Jennifer Moore-Mallinos
Illustration: Gustavo Mazali
Design and layout: Estudi Guasch, S.L.

All inquiries should be addressed to:
Barron's Educational Series, Inc.
250 Wireless Boulevard
Hauppauge, NY 11788
www.barronseduc.com

ISBN: 978-1-4380-0350-4
Library of Congress Control Number: 2013931784

Date of Manufacture: July 2013
Place of Manufacture: L. REX PRINTING COMPANY LIMITED,
Dongguan City, Guangdong, China

Product conforms to all applicable CPSC and CPSIA 2008 standards.
No lead or phthalate hazard.

Printed in China
9 8 7 6 5 4 3 2 1